CW00470414

Mindfulness for Children

A Beginners Guide to Mindfulness for Kids and Teens

Table of Contents

Introduction

Mindfulness is a meditation practice that when used appropriately or applied properly can heighten the qualities of awareness, like paying attention to your experience through the mind and senses; help kids not be judgmental, by observing with a neutral attitude and not labeling things as bad or good; stillness of the mind and heart, even if the body may be moving.

For adults, you may be tempted to use mindfulness as a tool for disciplining children, but mindfulness should not be used as an approach to demand a specific behavior from your child. Since mindfulness inherently embraces the qualities of acceptance, using it to achieve a specific behavior in your child defeats the purpose of this meditation.

I hope you will use this wonderful meditation approach to achieve a better way of life for your kid.

Chapter 1: Understanding Mindfulness for Your Kid

Did you know that the 'Father' of mindfulness meditation is Jon Kabat-Zinn? Yes, it was a molecular biologist, in the name of Jon Kabat-Zinn who introduced mindfulness meditation into the realms of medicine but without the accompanying Buddhism teachings. Mindfulness meditation was introduced as a stress reduction program in the University of Massachusetts Medical Center in 1979.

According to the founder, "mindfulness meditation is a moment-to-moment awareness cultivated by purposefully paying attention to things we ordinarily never give a moment's thought to. It is a systematic approach to developing new kinds of wisdom and control in our lives."

Fast forward to more than 30 years after the introduction of mindfulness meditation, a lot of research has shown evidence that by practicing mindfulness; you reap various psychological and physical health benefits. Mindfulness meditation is not focused on sitting rigidly on a lotus position as if you are the epitome of a Buddhist statue of meditation. In fact, it is more about living your life in the here and the now.

A Real-Life Example of Mindful Kids

There are a lot of school teachers who have turned to mindfulness meditation to reduce attention disorders, conflict, and anxiety in their classroom. In one perfect example is the class of teacher Steve Reidman at Toluca Lake Elementary School in Los Angeles.

Reidman was a fourth grade schoolteacher for over several years when he began experiencing classroom management problems, which became a first for him. He saw that quarrels in the playground were increasing and affecting the schoolchildren's ability to concentrate and settle down in class. That was when his friend Kaiser offered to teach mindfulness in his classroom.

According to teacher Reidman, he noticed a big difference in his classroom almost instantaneously. He noticed that the children were less anxious for a test and there was less conflict in the playground. Even with the way the kids walked to the classroom was different. Further, he also asked the children to do some mindfulness breathing right before their exams and their state test scores went up that year.

Although, Reidman believes that it is also because of his teaching skills that they were able to achieve higher score; but he also would like to attribute it to the kid's better state of mind brought about by mindfulness meditation. And this was years ago.

Currently, a lot of classes in the same school make use of mindfulness meditation. As one teacher asked the classroom of kids, 'what did you notice about your breath this morning?' Some children would respond 'it was like smoke' and another said 'mine was like a dragon.' And one 7-year old child summed up the experience by saying, 'I like the class because it makes me calm and soft inside.' It was also documented that after two to three weeks of mindfulness instruction, one classroom, which had the most number of behavioral problems as gauged by visits to the principal's office, progressed to having no behavioral problems.

In fact, in one second grade class, Emily was reported to verbalize that 'last week she made a drawing for her best friend, but her little brother tore it and that she was quite mad at him.' And she added that, she used deep breathing to calm herself and the good thing was, she got over her anger and realized that she could make the drawing again. This is such a huge leap of positive attitude from such a small person.

Based on further research, children and teacher interview, researchers have found that children who underwent mindfulness instructions were more attentive in class, less oppositional toward teachers, and less aggressive. With children interviews, kids have reported that they are feeling more positive emotions like optimism. And based on teacher observations, the kids were more introspective than those who were not instructed in mindfulness meditation.

The Benefits of Mindfulness

There are so many benefits that we can reap from mindfulness. In this subchapter, we will be basing the stated benefits of mindfulness in scientific and parallel studies.

Acceptance

One of the components of mindfulness training is acceptance, where it is non-judgmental. It is like an observance of the here and now, taking note of what's really happening without identifying each item or action as good or bad. In clinical and medical populations, mindfulness training includes acceptance of emotions, thoughts, worries, and pain without trying to change, avoid, or escape them. Since the individuals are willing to stay with the negative emotions and pain, they benefit more because of a greater sense of self-acceptance.

Relaxation

We have to emphasize that mindfulness is not the same as relaxation and nor is relaxation the goal of mindfulness. To reiterate, the goal of mindfulness is living in the here and the now, a moment by moment of purposeful awareness. However, through meditation a person does become relaxed. Often, researchers observe that there is a decrease in heart rate, breathing and muscle tension because of practicing mindfulness which also slows down racing thoughts just by taking time to observe each thought.

Self-Management

Mindfulness in itself is already a self-management intervention. In self-awareness of a pattern or problem the first step is change. Just by sitting down and focusing your attention and awareness on the moment and of the moment that the urges emerge, the stressors and triggers of the urge can also come into focus which will assist in an active problem solving. This is especially useful in people who are facing addiction and behavioral problems like substance abuser and bulimic person.

Cognitive Change

Cognitive change can also be achieved through mindfulness meditation. It can lead to changes in the attitude of one's thoughts and even in thought patterns. Take for example, just because you are scared of monsters in the dark, do not necessarily mean there are really monsters there or just because you think that you are a failure does not make it so. Once you realize and accept this concept, cognitive change happens.

Health Benefits

So far there have been recorded observations of the benefits entailed with a mindfulness meditation therapy or training. Various health benefits were seen and recorded but specific scientific reasons for the changes have not yet been looked into deeper. Examples of the health benefits reaped by mindfulness meditation practitioners were: reduced cholesterol levels, a reduction in blood pressure, alleviate depression and other mental illness (eating disorders, post-traumatic stress syndrome, anxiety and more), improved ability to handle stress, and a reduction in chronic pain.

Benefits for Children

Currently, there are few studies that really looked into the benefits of mindfulness training in children. So, far here is what they have learned and observed when it comes to mindfulness benefits for children:

- As we have mentioned earlier, there was one classroom full of children who benefitted from mindfulness training with a positive behavioral change as gauged by the student's visit to the principal's office.
- In one study conducted by UCLA, they found that mindfulness meditation positively helps teenagers battle with Attention Deficit Hyperactivity Disorder (ADHD) by increasing their ability to focus and reducing their anxiety levels.
- In one of the classroom examples we have cited above, it was found out that mindfulness meditation helps children lessen their anxiety for a test and they have also appeared to do better in their exam results.

So far, as experts in the field have put it, there's still so much to be done and studies to really know the depths of how mindfulness can benefit a child. Most studies available are based on adults and it has shown to be beneficial for adults in terms of increasing happiness, health, decreasing depressing, and stress— now, wouldn't it be plain selfish to withhold these wonderful benefits from children?

Further, experts also speculate and wonder if the benefits of mindfulness can help preschoolers learn to regulate their behaviors and their emotions in order to be successful all throughout their schooling years. Further, they also wonder if mindfulness can help children all throughout their life and if it could protect them against future mental illnesses in the future. All of these possibilities are being looked forward to with optimism since responses to the program are positive and little resistance was encountered when the mindfulness program was introduced.

Chapter 2: Teaching Mindfulness to Children

Now that you know more what mindfulness meditation is and how it helps children and its benefits. Let us now begin mindfulness practices with children. In this chapter, you will be taught the process, techniques, and various mindfulness exercises that you can teach children to practice.

Tips before You Begin Teaching

Here are some helpful tips to help you get started on the right track when it comes to teaching children mindfulness meditation.

Practice Mindfulness Meditation

Just like any great teacher or leader, they will tell you that it pays to be experienced and knowledgeable on the craft that you are teaching. Therefore, practice mindfulness meditation yourself. Learn the ropes before teaching it to children. This will make you more effective in teaching mindfulness meditation because you can only offer what you yourself have cultivated.

Daily Practice

Since humans are creature of habits, it is only prudent and effective to practice daily so that you can incorporate mindfulness meditation into your daily activities and soon it will be a part of a lifelong habit.

Setting a Time For Mindfulness

It is also logical to practice mindfulness at a certain time of the day and stick to it. This is especially useful for children because it helps them settle down.

Involve the Child

Involve your child in the mindfulness meditation activities. This will help them be more active in the process and not just a mere spectator. If you are teaching several kids, then rotate the schedule for who gets to operate the mindfulness bell, that way everybody can participate. Pretty soon, everybody is clamoring for mindfulness meditation as you begin to practice it daily.

Share Your Experience

Since children respond well when we share our experiences, then you can share with the children your experiences with mindfulness meditation. You can tell stories of how you have used mindfulness meditation in your life, in times of stress or how it had uplifted your mood and spirits. By hearing your experiences, the child can learn from this and will also draw from your experiences and apply it to their use of mindfulness meditation.

Let the Children Share Their Experience

A lot of youngsters love sharing their experiences. Let them share what they have experience or notice during mindfulness meditation—whether they find it distracting or challenging. Through sharing, it opens your eyes and the other children's eyes on what they can experience, achieve or notice while under mindfulness, on which you or they wouldn't have noticed if left on their own devices.

Create the Environment

One of the keys to a successful mindfulness meditation is setting up your surroundings. Remember, you are dealing with children here and they have a very short span of attention. In order to make it easy for them to concentrate on the meditation at hand, clear up the space you have chosen for the meditation. Further, by setting up the space you are sending a message that mindfulness meditation is a special time. Also, remind the children to refrain from talking, fidgeting, or even take a bathroom break in the midst of mindfulness meditation. Clear the clutter too, so that it is easier to clear your mind of thoughts except for the task at hand which is mindfulness meditation.

Helpful Script and Instruction

I have included below a mindfulness meditation script and instruction that you can use in your daily mindfulness lesson with children. Once you are more adept in teaching or more comfortable with teaching children mindfulness meditation, you can get creative.

1) Ask the children to sit still, with eyes closed, upper body upright, and keep quiet. Tell the kids that this will be known as the 'mindful bodies' pose. When you say these two words, it means that they have to sit still, eyes closed, upper body upright, and quiet.

2) Tell the kids to keep all their focus on the sound that they are about to hear and listen to it until it is gone completely.

3) Use a rainstick or a bell that has a sustained sound which will encourage mindful listening in kids. Then begin by ringing the bell or rainstick. In succeeding mindfulness meditation exercises, you can allow a child to ring the bell. If you are teaching a lot of children, have them take turns in ringing the bell.

4) Again, remind the kids to concentrate on the sound.

5) Instruct the kids to raise his or her hand once he or she can no longer hear the bell ringing.

6) Wait for majority of the kids to raise their hands. Anticipate that the kid or kids will not be raising their hands simultaneously. Once majority of the children have raised their hands, prompt them to mindfully and slowly move their raised hands down to their chest or stomach and feel their breathing.

7) To help the kids focusing their attention, you can say breathing reminders like 'breathing in... breathing out...'

8) To end the session, ring the bell.

Chapter 3: Various Ways to Teach Children Mindfulness

As we have seen above, the mindfulness practice for children is not quite dissimilar in adult practice. With children, you just need to be more creative to hold their attention and anticipate roadblocks to attention and remove them prior to the practice. In order for our mindfulness teaching to be effective we need to be aware of what the experience of a child is like. This will make it easy for us to pattern mindfulness exercises. Children's thoughts and perceptions are more concrete rather than abstract, that's why the mindfulness activity instructions should be descriptive, concrete, and clear. It has to be descriptive because children's imaginations are quite creative. Adding humor to your activity also helps.

If it was not mentioned before, then it is best to mention it now, when starting your very first mindfulness training with a child, success is important. Thus, start with something short and simple. If for an adult, 15 minutes of meditation is nothing out of the ordinary, but for a child this can be like an eternity and may affect his or her future perception of mindfulness meditation. So keep it short, a maximum of 5 minutes will more than suffice.

Mindfulness of the Environment Exercises

The best way to introduce children to mindfulness is to use the environment. Direct the child's focus to his or her environment. Through the environment, you can point out the need for mindfulness by revealing what they are aware of and what they are not aware of.

Object Awareness

To start this mindfulness exercise, begin by asking the child to draw an object. It can be a clock, scissors, shoe, cellphone, table, etc. As the child begins to draw the object of their focus, remind them that the activity is not about how well the child drew the object. This is an important process because the child might get frustrated with their drawing ability. Just tell them to draw as best as they can.

After drawing, let the child shift their attention to the actual object at hand and focus on the minute details. After several minutes of inspection, let the child draw the object again, this time in a separate paper and taking into focus the added details he or she has learned about the object of their focus.

When done drawing a second time, allow them to compare their first and second drawings. Ask the children to identify missing pieces in their first drawing that they drew in the second drawing. In almost all cases, the second drawing will be more life-like and accurate with pieces that they never took the time to notice.

Self-Awareness in the Environment

The second activity in environment mindfulness is awareness of the self within your surroundings. In this exercise you are helping the child to pay purposeful attention to both his or her actions and the environment, instead of going through the day like a robot. This could be done in a fun and enjoyable manner by asking the child to pretend that they are a journalist. They need to cover their own experience for the day and writing down the day's experience as it is happening. For younger children who don't yet know how to write, they can ask their parent's to write it down for them or have them record the happenings on the phone.

What to write down in their journals, ask the kids to write down the step by step happenings of their day. What they did when they woke up. At first just begin by focusing their writing on the first hour of the day. Let them record their experiences in the journal daily.

After a week of journaling, let them read their experiences from day one and they will notice that each day their self and environment awareness continued to grow. Example, maybe in day 1 they just wrote, I woke up, went to the bathroom, and brushed my teeth. Maybe the next day she or he added newer activities like eating breakfast, dressing up, etc. Then slowly more details cropped up in their writing like what she or he ate for breakfast, how she or he chose their clothes for the day, and so on.

If the child has difficulty at any point, encourage them by asking questions that would provide more details. Like, how did you feel when you brushed your teeth? How did the cold shirt felt against your skin? How did the toothpaste tasted?

Mindfulness of the Body Exercises

Once the child you are teaching about mindfulness masters the art of environment mindfulness, he or she is ready to begin doing mindfulness of the body exercises. This step entails being purposefully aware of their experiences within their body. This is a significant aspect of mindfulness since enhanced body awareness directs to a fuller self-awareness.

The Raisin Meditation: Focusing On the Senses

What's exciting about this exercise is that this is the exact replica of the first mindfulness meditation training used by Kabat-Zinn in his very first mindfulness program. It is quite straightforward and does not require much adaptation for it to be used by children. The exercise is centered on being conscious of an object in the environment.

In this specific exercise, each child is given three raisins. The child is asked to be aware of his or her own experience with the raisin. Awareness should be focused on nonjudgmental experience of the child about the raisin. Maybe in your next mindfulness meditation exercise you can pick a different food item like popcorn, chocolate, or whatever it is that you deem would be interesting to the child. Do not repeat this mindfulness meditation too much or else you risk the exercise from becoming uninteresting and repetitive for the child and consequently they may lose the goal of mindfulness.

One of the best ways to go about this meditation exercise is to read the script below, with a calm and slow yet appropriately loud voice. These texts were taken directly from Kabat-Zinn's mindfulness training.

Bring your attention to the raisin, observing it carefully as if you had never seen one before. Pick up one raisin and feel its texture between your fingers and notice its colors. Be aware of any thoughts you might be having about the raisin. Note any thoughts or feelings of liking or disliking raisins if they come up while you are looking at it. Then lift the raisin to your nose and smell it for a while and finally, with awareness, bring it to your lips, being aware of the arm moving the hand to position it correctly and of your mouth salivating as the mind and body anticipate eating. Take the raisin into your mouth and chew it slowly, experiencing the actual taste of the raisin. Hold it in your mouth. When you feel ready to swallow, watch the impulse to swallow as it comes up, so that even that is experienced consciously. When you are ready, pick up the second raisin and repeat this process, with a new raisin, as if it is now the first raisin you have ever seen.

Breathing Meditation

Fundamental to mindfulness is the breathing meditation because it improves the concentration on the here and now experience. If this breathing meditation exercise is accomplished properly, then that means that the child is aware only of the here and now. Since the focus of each breathing meditation exercise is the current breath and not the breath before it nor the breath after it. This breathing meditation exercise has a calming effect on the body and mind.

In order for the breathing meditation exercises to be done properly, you have to show the child how to breathe properly. Youngsters especially, may not have enough presence of mind to really pay attention to breathing before since it is a natural body function which they may have taken for granted. Start by demonstrating and verbalizing how the cool air enters the nose and how the warm air is exhaled. The importance in the breathing meditation is just to be aware and not about changing the natural rhythm of breathing, pushing out your breath, or holding it.

To help children focus on their breathing, allow them to count their breaths. This can be done in various ways like saying the word one as they inhale and repeating the same number as they exhale before proceeding to the next number in the next breath cycle. Count up to five and then return back to one. If it is hard for them to focus on their breathing whilst counting, you can just let them say the word one for each inhale and exhale without moving on to the next number.

Again, as the breathing meditation is ongoing gently remind the kids that if their minds wander to other thoughts aside from their breathing, just take note of what the thought is about and gently return back to meditating on their breaths.

The kids that you are teaching will be amazed at the effort needed to focus their attention on their breaths and keeping it focused. Therefore, begin your first breathing session for a short period, around five breath cycles. As you continue to practice the breathing meditation exercise, you can gradually increase the breath cycles. If you find that the child gets frustrated with the attempt at concentrating on their breath, just gently encourage them to keep trying. Let them know that distracting thoughts and feelings are natural and should not be viewed negatively. In time, they will learn to master this breathing meditation exercise. Also encourage the children to make use of this mindfulness technique when they are feeling angry, overwhelmed, or anxious. They can also apply this breathing technique just before an exam to help them keep a focused mind while answering test questions. The breathing technique is also helpful in putting themselves to sleep.

The Consciousness for Movement Exercise

In this mindfulness exercise the children are purposefully focusing their attention to their body as they interact with the environment. If you are doing this exercise with several children, ensure that you have a big room that is large enough for the children to move around unimpeded and safely. This is an important aspect of the exercise so that the children can remain attentive to their own experience. To make the exercise a bit more enjoyable, you can play soothing music in the background.

To begin this mindfulness exercise, direct the children to move around the room in the softest manner as they can. Let them imagine that they are walking on a delicate glass floor or on egg shells, that's why they need to carry their feet and walk around as quietly as possible. Ask the children to focus their attention on their calf muscle as it tightens to move their foot off the ground and as they set it slowly back down in front of them. Also allow them to also focus their attention on their hands floating beside their body, in space. Allow them to focus on one leg at a time for a few steps then changing their focus to the other leg and then changing their focus on their arms. Tell the children that if their thoughts wander to other thoughts aside from the task at hand, let them take not of what those thoughts were, and slowly return their consciousness to the here and now—to the task at hand, to a part of their body their leg or arm.

Mindfulness Meditation

At this point in the mindfulness exercises this is better suited to older children. The exercises included here focuses on the meditation bubble and experiencing the here and now with an emphasis on non-engagement of thoughts.

The Visualization Meditation

This mindfulness exercise encourages imagination and creativity. It is most helpful for children who are feeling anxious since this exercise is linked with visualization for relaxation. Here are the steps to follow:

1) With shoulders relaxed and back straight, sit in a comfortable position and close your eyes.

2) Allow your mind to be free of thoughts and keep it blank.
3) Once your mind is blank, start by imagining yourself in a place that you find relaxing, safe, and comfortable. This can be your own bed, a lake, beach, mountain or whatever place that gives you a sense of a safe haven.
4) Slowly imagine the place transform right in front of you, getting clearer by the minute.
5) Look to your right. What do you see?
6) What about to your left? What can you see?
7) Take in all the details of your safe haven.
8) Take a deep breath. Do you smell anything?
9) Imagine yourself walking around your safe haven as you look at specific things in your safe haven.
10) Keep your focus in your safe haven and note how you are feeling.
11) If you find your thoughts wandering out of focus, take a mental note of what they are and slowly return your mind back into focus.
12) After a time, place your hand in front of your eyes and open your eyes.
13) Slowly spread out your fingers to let the light stream in between.
14) When you are ready, slowly move your hand away from your eyes.

Meditation on The Bubble

This mindfulness exercise focuses awareness on not engaging thoughts, letting go, and the thinking process. The goal of this exercise is to help children slow down and observe their thoughts, then letting go or releasing these thoughts without judgment.

To go about this exercise, read the script out loud in a calm and soothing voice. Then let the child continue the exercise in silence for a few more minutes or let him or her set the pace.

1) Start at a sitting pose with shoulders relaxed, back straight, and position yourself comfortable.
2) Gently close your eyes.
3) Slowly imagine bubbles rising up in front of you.
4) Imagine that each bubble contains perception, feeling or thought.
5) See the first bubble rise up, what is inside it?
6) Closely look at the thought, observe it, and watch as it floats slowly away from you.
7) Then try not to think, evaluate, or judge the thought more deeply.
8) Once the first bubble floats out of sight, imagine the second bubbly floating up.
9) What is inside the bubble? Watch and observe the bubble as it floats slowly away from you.

10) If your mind is blank as a bubble floats up, then just see the bubble as blank inside until it floats slowly away from you.

Conclusion

So you see, teaching mindfulness meditation to children is easy and achievable. It is also a wonderful and productive way of spending quality time with your child while teaching them about the perks of living in the moment. Further, together you and your child are sharing in a healthy past time where various psychological and health benefits are being enjoyed by both you and your child's mind and body.

For teachers who are dealing with children most days of the week, teaching them mindfulness meditation is a good way to help them deal with stress, negative emotions, and conflict. As we have mentioned, mindfulness has been shown to help school children do better in their studies while becoming well-behaved and with lesser opposition against their teachers.

All in all, mindfulness for children is an easy and enjoyable technique that promotes relaxation and a better state of mind for the little ones.

The ideas, concepts, and opinions expressed in this book are intended to be used for educational and reference purposes only. Author and publisher claim no responsibility to any person or entity for any liability, loss, or damage caused or alleged to be caused directly or indirectly as a result of the use, application, or interpretation of the material in this book.

Printed in Great Britain
by Amazon